AUSTRALIA IN COLOUR

PHOTOGRAPHS FROM THE AUSTRALIAN GEOGRAPHIC IMAGE COLLECTION

CONTENTS

OPPOSITE: *Devils Marbles, NT.* BARRY SKIPSEY

Hundreds of granite boulders up to 6m in diameter have been sculpted
by wind and rain into rounded shapes that glow late in the day.

Spider Gorge, Mornington station, Kimberley, WA. NICK RAINS

This former cattle station is now a private nature reserve edged by the rugged
King Leopold Ranges and sprinkled with magnificent gorges, creek lines and gullies.

INTRODUCTION

Australia basks in colourful brushstrokes, from the brilliant blues of the ocean to the deep reds of the desert, from the gold of bright wattle to the green of our lush forests.

AUSTRALIA is the variegated continent. Indeed, no other country on Earth is more lavishly hued. This vibrancy is not just on show in the jaunty flourish of our birds and flowers; it seems to radiate from the depths of the earth and sky, from the forests, deserts and seas.

Time has been the artist at work. Across the land lie surfaces that have been scoured, doused and baked — some for more than 100 million years. By this alchemy the elements have created an astonishing palette.

Everywhere you look the brushstrokes are bold. So it's little wonder that the pigments that energise the land should also inspire the art traditions of the world's oldest continuous culture. From ancient paintings adorning natural rock shelters, to elaborate works on bark and the striking dot designs of the inland deserts, Aboriginal art celebrates country in earthy, luminous shades.

These traditions invite us to recognise colours not simply within a scene but as the signatures of a much larger canvas. Australia expresses tonal vigour on a colossal scale: vast red dune-ridge deserts mottled with tawny spinifex; hundreds of kilometres of biscuit-coloured sandstone escarpments; entire coastlines where turquoise waters lap tropical reefs and islands; millions of square kilometres of blindingly white salt lakes. Such brilliance is accentuated by the clarity of the air and the cutting sharpness of the light. Even at night, these southern heavens seem blacker and the glinting stars more mesmerising.

Above all else, Australia's climate makes colour a moveable feast — or famine. To the standard quartet of seasons add fire, flood and drought. This trio are the old masters of turmoil, etching the landscape in bleached, dusty browns, and charcoal blacks before the big downpours come to slap on a fresh coat of green. To be Australian is to live a colourful life. Here, hope, fear and joy come in many tints. We are a vivid work in progress.

RED

From the rusty hues of the desert dirt to the colourings on our native flora and fauna, red is the colour of the Australian outback.

HEAD INLAND from our mainland coast and sooner or later every road ends up on a red dirt track barrelling straight to the horizon. Chances are you'll have passed rusty sheds and red gums, mobs of red cattle, white utes steeped in red-dust stains and sunsets that flare with a molten glow.

Red is the outback's cardinal colour. It's always there, whether you're trekking Kings Canyon, or climbing a Simpson Desert dune, or deep in a Pilbara Gorge, or admiring a Kakadu rock shelter. It's impossible to imagine these landmarks — or journeys like the Canning Stock Route — in anything but those gritty, burnished shades of ferric red, terracotta and deep ochre orange.

Australian nature's never shy with red. Flashes appear on our parrots and cockatoos, the red kangaroo, and the redback spider. It's there in quangdong fruit and brilliant blooms like the waratah, bottlebrush and Sturt's desert pea.

OPPOSITE: **Swamp bloodwood blooms. NT.** DAVID HANCOCK

The large flowers of this showy tree come in various hues from white to pink to crimson. It naturally occurs from the Kimberley to the northern reaches of the NT.

Lunette, Mungo National Park, NSW. BARRY SKIPSEY

Pitted and wrinkled by run-off, this lunette marks the relict eastern shore of a body
of fresh water and holds some of the earliest evidence of modern humans.

Bungle Bungles, Purnululu National Park, WA. NICK RAINS

The towering, striped beehive formations of the eastern Kimberley morph through
an explosion of colours at dawn and dusk — oranges, reds, purples and crimson.

Sturt's desert pea, near Lake Eyre, SA. NICK RAINS

Fire-engine red, the flowers of the floral emblem of SA are up to 9cm long
and found widely across the sunburned central arid regions of Australia.

Mountain ash, Styx Valley, Tas. BILL BACHMAN

The gnarled, moss-draped bark of this 84m old-growth eucalypt, known locally as
'Gandalf's Staff,' lies within the 'Tolkien Track' area of Tasmania's Styx Valley.

Millstream Chichester National Park, WA.

NICK RAINS

Flushed red and orange with iron, the cliffs over Python Pool dwarf a lone swimmer in this stunning Pilbara landscape.

Red** Siphonogorgia **sea fan, Great Barrier Reef, Qld. MIKE MCCOY

Sea fans, which can reach a spread of several metres, typically grow in abundance on
reef walls or drop-offs, especially where ocean currents are at their strongest.

Hermit crab, Cocos (Keeling) Islands, Indian Ocean. DON FUCHS

With such vivid hues, hordes of hermit crabs provide a colourful moving contrast
to the coarse creamy sands and turquoise water of the Cocos (Keeling) Islands.

Dust storm, Hay Plain, NSW. THOMAS WIELECKI

Our ancient, arid and windy continent produces a lot of dust, and, exacerbated by drought
and westerly winds, seasonal dust storms can turn the evening sky blood red.

West of the Flinders Ranges, SA. MIKE LANGFORD
Wind has raked mesmerising patterns into this sienna dune, studded with
hardy plants, on the arid west side of the Flinders Ranges.

Newhaven station, NT.

BARRY SKIPSEY

The desert's palette of rich red sand and eye-searingly white salt pan is perfectly captured at Lake Bennett in Australia's red centre.

BLUE

Exploring Australia's wild blue yonder takes travellers from the aqua depths off our stunning beaches to the wide skies that stand over our deserts.

AUSTRALIA HAS a love affair with blue. It's synonymous with our outdoor life and the wild blue yonder. We go bush for the breezy freedom of wide plains where toothy ranges stand tall against bold cobalt skies.

Back on the coast, access to water of every shade — from pale aqua to inky indigo — is considered a birthright. It's the backdrop colour of summer and endless childhood days mucking around in rockpools, fishing off jetties and riding waves to shore.

No surprise then that this is the hue evoking space, openness and a wry, egalitarian spirit. We'll always be as good as the next bloke — but never a better mate than his blue heeler. The ultimate Australian accolade? To be true blue.

By contrast, out bush a burst of blue can be rare, even oddly menacing — be it a blue-tongue lizard's angry gape or a cassowary's icy stare. Worse still, the seaside sting of a bluebottle jellyfish or blue-ringed octopus. Thank goodness for the chirpy woodland antics of our superb fairy wrens.

OPPOSITE: **Rossiter Bay, near Esperance, WA.** EDWARD STOKES

Grey granite boulders form punctuation marks in the flowing turquoise poetry of WA's southern coastline.

Tom Groggin station, NSW. ROSS DUNSTAN

Shrouded in a pale blue gauze of early morning mist, Tom Groggin station
sits snugly beside the Alpine Way, on the NSW–Victoria border.

Watsons Crags and Mt Sentinel, NSW. ROSS DUNSTAN

Near the Australian mainland's highest peaks, the slopes around Watsons Crags,
seen here from Muellers Peak, are among the steepest in the Snowies.

Lake Eyre, SA. NICK RAINS

On average, Lake Eyre South and North only flood twice a century, but partially
fill every 5–10 years, providing a mirror that stretches to the horizon.

Lake Malata, SA. EDWARD STOKES

A milky blue sky, with just a few flecks of white, shines over the glistening
salt ridges of Lake Malata, 60km north-west of Port Lincoln.

Cape Range National Park, WA.

ANDREW GREGORY

This remote park is located on a 200km-long promontory shaped like a beckoning finger jutting into the cobalt-blue Indian Ocean.

Lake Mulwala, NSW/Vic. BILL BACHMAN

Drowned gum trees poke out of Lake Mulwala, one of the controlled waters on the Murray River.
It was formed when Yarrawonga Weir was constructed in the 1930s.

Delisser Sandhills, WA. MITCH REARDON

Propelled by strong winds and a steady sand supply, giant white dunes
on the Nullarbor coastline engulf everything in their path.

Sugarloaf Rock, near Cape Naturaliste, WA. ANDREW GREGORY

Limestone bluffs, boulders and sea caves make up the coastline around
Cape Naturaliste, on the wild south-west coast of WA.

King Island, Tas. ROB WALLS

Bass Strait's swells pound into the jagged King Island coastline
in an explosion of seaspray, surge and spume.

Direction Island, Cocos (Keeling) Islands, Indian Ocean. DON FUCHS

Green turtles and tall-fin batfish glide in the postcard-perfect water under the
Direction Island jetty. It's visited by about 100 round-the-world yachts each year.

Wistari Reef, Qld. MIKE MCCOY

Myriad coral reefs form a maze of blue and green hues in the lagoon on
Wistari Reef, part of the 2000km-long Great Barrier Reef.

GREEN

It is the colour of our lush forests and the flocks of our wild budgies, but green promises the great dream for farmers — reprieve from the drought.

THE PRODIGAL colour, the one tint Australians can never take for granted. Through the depths of drought, green becomes a tease, a chimera, a memory. Some farm kids turn 10 before they see their home patch really flourishing. Even in less severe spells, a tinge of new growth can come and go before summer finally loosens its grip and the rains set in. Up north the spring months brood and linger until the monsoon's sway makes the savannah country lush once more.

Meanwhile those great survivors — the eucalypts — bide their time. Their sparse, waxy-leafed canopies bestow much of the Australian bush with a muted green that has a silvery blue tinge. Only in the moist mountain valleys and pockets of coastal rainforest do the classic forest and fern greens flaunt their wares.

Elsewhere, green hangs on by working the margins — stoic paperbarks along dry creek beds, mangroves fringing tidal channels on hard-baked flood plains and old coolibahs shoulder to shoulder beside outback billabongs.

Yet, every few years, there will be a season when the rains just keep on coming and the inland cops a thorough soaking. It's then that green is the livery of desert miracles, as brilliant and fleeting as a wheeling flock of wild budgies.

OPPOSITE: **Gum leaves.** CHRISSIE GOLDRICK

Eucalypts are the scent, shade and shape of the Australian bush and we can boast more than 900 species. Only 10—12 of the world's eucalypt species are not endemic to Australia.

Table Cape, Tas. BILL BACHMAN

Rectangles of white pyrethrum daisies stand out in the multicoloured
agricultural patchwork of north-western Tasmania.

Tweed Valley, NSW. NICK RAINS

The rim of this ancient volcanic caldera can be seen on the horizon giving
way to a large, fertile valley through which snakes the Tweed River.

Mossman River, Qld.

ANDREW GREGORY

In the lush shaded rainforest of the Daintree, the surging Mossman River occasionally quietens to emerald pools studded with granite boulders.

Mitchell River silt jetties, Gippsland Lakes, Vic. DON FUCHS

These silt jetties are the second largest in the world after those of the Mississippi River and
are formed by silt washed down by the Mitchell River system over a million years.

Maria Island, Tas. DON FUCHS

Across sparkling turquoise waters, charter operator Jim Ransley
ferries walkers ashore for a guided three-day walk on Maria Island.

Millstream Chichester National Park, WA.

NICK RAINS

Crossing Pool is a spring-fed oasis in the Pilbara fringed by paperbarks, shady palms, reeds and river red gums.

Mueller River, Croajingolong National Park, Vic. RORY MCGUINNESS

Stained tea-brown by the tannins in decaying vegetation, the Mueller River winds
its way through tall stringybarks and thick underbrush in wild East Gippsland.

Cooper Creek Wilderness, Qld. BRIAN CASSEY

Towering fan palms create an aerial mosiac in the Daintree, northern Queensland.
The rainforest here has changed little in 130 million years.

Border Ranges National Park, NSW.

NICK RAINS

Gnarled, twisted and covered in mosses and lichens, these Antarctic beech trees grow 1000m up the extinct Tweed volcano in northern NSW.

GOLD

Like warm sunshine, gold is close to the Australian heart, whether pinned with a sprig of wattle or swelling with pride at claiming an Olympic victory.

IT GROWS in every corner of the continent. With nigh on a thousand species there's always one in flower. More than just Australia's floral emblem, the gold radiance of the humble wattle has become the hue that unifies a nation, a symbol of commemoration, harvest bounty and sporting triumph: "Gold! Gold to Australia! Gold!"

Down south, wattle blossom is the harbinger of spring, a welcome dollop of sunny colour. Across every habitat gold also has its feathered envoys — yellow robins, pardalotes, golden whistlers, honeyeaters, and those larrikin loudmouths the sulphur-crested cockatoos.

Through the cooler months, soft sunshine brings a warm cast to our beaches and dunescapes. In sandstone country like the Blue Mountains and central Queensland, low-angled winter light fills the pale cliffs and hollowed overhangs with a honey-tinged glow. Then by spring's end, Australia's huge tracts of grassland and cropping country are vast swaying seas of pale, spun gold.

In its most sublime expression gold is the 24-carat currency of the arriving dawn and sunset's afterglow. In moments shared on verandahs, or beside a waterhole the world is on hold as everything is bathed in the quiet, gilded light.

OPPOSITE: **West Wyalong wattle.** ESTHER BEATON

Golden wattles blanket Australia from east to west and were proclaimed as our national floral emblem in 1988. Wattle Day is gazetted as 1 September each year.

Ghost gum, Newhaven station, NT.

Nicknamed 'Elephant Tree', this twisted ghost gum provides vital habitat for the
myriad birds that occur on Birds Australia's NT reserve, Newhaven station.

Burra, SA. JAMES MCCORMACK

Angled sun lends its golden tinge to this paddock and abandoned
residence near Burra, 140km north of Adelaide.

Pear-fruited mallee. BILL BACHMAN

Limited to the western part of the northern Western Australian wheatbelt, this eucalypt species has a distinctive salmon red-coloured bark and these spectacularly hued blooms.

Cradle Mountain–Lake St Clair National Park, Tas. JASON EDWARDS

The 5–7mm crinkly leaves of the nothofagus, or deciduous beech, set hills
ablaze with colour in Tasmania's central highlands each autumn.

Yarrawonga, Vic.

BILL BACHMAN

In autumn, this abandoned poplar plantation explodes into rich gold and yellow tones. Poplars were originally cultivated for matchwood.

Dunns Swamp, Blue Mountains, NSW. DON FUCHS

As the sun rises behind Mt Midderula, it burns the mist
from Dunns Swamp and burnishes it in bronze.

Python Pool, Millstream Chichester National Park, WA. NICK RAINS

Set ablaze, as if lit from the inside, these cliffs cool their toes and
reflect their glory in the tranquil waters of Python Pool.

Warrumbungle National Park, NSW. GRAHAME MCCONNELL

Like threads across a rumpled canvas, ridge lines and mist lines interweave in
this view from Siding Spring Mountain, 350km north-west of Sydney.

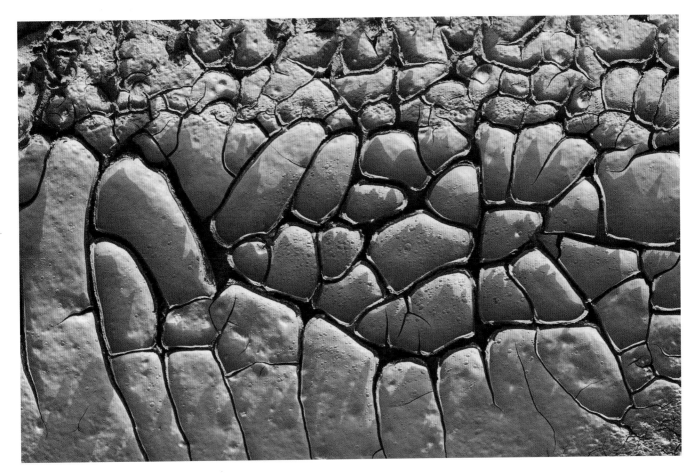

Dry waterhole, Corner Country, NSW. MITCH REARDON

With an average rainfall of 200mm, this is the driest area of the driest inhabited continent.
As drought develops, waterholes and their sun-tortured beds turn to cracked, dried mud.

Ephemeral lake, near Lake Gregory, WA.

ANDREW GREGORY

Between the Great Sandy and Tanami deserts, this unnamed lake is usually a salt pan but here reflects the heaven's splendour.

AUSTRALIA IN COLOUR

PHOTOGRAPHS FROM THE AUSTRALIAN GEOGRAPHIC IMAGE COLLECTION

All the photographs featured in this book can be ordered as high quality photographic prints.
For details and prices, please visit **www.australiangeographicprints.com.au**

AUSTRALIAN GEOGRAPHIC EDITOR IN CHIEF: Chrissie Goldrick
BOOK DESIGN: Mike Rossi WRITERS: Quentin Chester, Chrissie Goldrick, Ken Eastwood
SUB-EDITOR: Josephine Sargent PROOFREADER: Nina Paine
PRODUCTION MANAGER: Victoria Jefferys PREPRESS: Klaus Müller

BAUER MEDIA CEO: David Goodchild
AUSTRALIAN GEOGRAPHIC PUBLISHER: Jo Runciman
PUBLISHER, SPECIALIST DIVISION: Cornelia Schulze

First printed in 2011; reprinted in 2015
Printed in China by Leo Paper Products

© Bauer Media 2015

Published by Bauer Media, 54–58 Park Street, Sydney, NSW 2000
Australian Geographic customer service 1300 555 176 (Australia only)
www.australiangeographic.com.au

AUTHOR: Chester, Quentin.
TITLE: Australia in colour : images from the Australian Geographic image collection / Quentin Chester, Chrissie Goldrick.
ISBN: 9781742452272 (hbk.)
SUBJECTS: Australian Geographic Pty. Ltd.--Pictorial works. Photography in geography. Australia--Pictorial works.
OTHER AUTHORS/CONTRIBUTORS: Goldrick, Chrissie.
DEWEY NUMBER: 910.9

Other titles in the series Photographs from the Australian Geographic Image Collection:
Landscapes of Australia

FRONT COVER:
Newhaven station, NT.
BARRY SKIPSEY

The desert's palette of rich red sand and eye-searingly white salt pan is perfectly captured at Lake Bennett in Australia's red centre.

TITLE PAGE:
West MacDonnell Ranges, NT.
BARRY SKIPSEY

Sunset paints the cliffs of the Heavitree Range in shades of red and purple highlighting the different plant communities that provide such a diversity of habitats for the rich wildlife of the 'West Macs'.

BACK COVER:
Mossman River, Qld.
ANDREW GREGORY

In the lush shaded rainforest of the Daintree, the surging Mossman River occasionally quietens to emerald pools studded with granite boulders.